Enid Blyton

BIBLE STORIES

David the Shepherd Boy

ILLUSTRATED BY STEPHANIE McFETRIDGE BRITT

First published in 1996 by Candle
Books. Distributed by SP Trust Ltd,
Triangle Business Park, Wendover
Road, Aylesbury, Bucks HP22 5BL,
England

ISBN 1 85985 100 2

Designed and created by
Three's Company,
5 Dryden Street,
London WC2E 9NW

Illustrations by Stephanie
McFetridge Britt

Worldwide co-edition organised and
produced by
Angus Hudson Ltd,
Concorde House,
Grenville Place,
London NW7 3SA
Phone +44 181 959 3668
Fax + 44 181 959 3678

Printed in Singapore

David the Shepherd Boy

The king of Israel was Saul, whom the old priest Samuel had chosen to rule over the people. For some years the king pleased Samuel, and then he quarrelled bitterly with him.

Samuel went away, sorry he had chosen such a king for his people.

One day the voice of God came to Samuel.

'Go to Bethlehem, to Jesse's house. I have chosen a king from his sons.'

So Samuel went to the city of Bethlehem.

'Do you come in peace?' asked the watchman.

'I come to hold a feast,' said Samuel. 'Go to Jesse. Tell him he is to come, and bring his sons with him.'

The man went and told Jesse. Jesse was a farmer, and he felt glad that such a great man as Samuel should ask for him. So he and his sons dressed in their best clothes and went to the place where the feast was to be held.

Samuel was there, waiting, for he knew God had chosen one of Jesse's sons to be king.

'Tell your sons to come before me,' said Samuel. So the young men stood in front of him, strong, fully-grown and good to look at. Samuel wondered which was to be king. He looked at each carefully.

But God spoke to him, 'Not this one. Nor is this the one, nor even this one.' It seemed as if not one of Jesse's sons was to be chosen after all.

Samuel was puzzled. Then he turned to Jesse. 'Are all your sons here?' he asked.

'All but one, and he is only a boy,' said Jesse. 'He guards the sheep. He is too young to come to the feast.'

'Bring him here,' said Samuel. So one of the brothers went to fetch the boy. His name was David, and he was the youngest. He sat guarding the sheep, singing in the sunshine.

He was not very old, but his face was brown and healthy, and his voice was sweet when he sang. He

could make music too, and everyone loved him.
   'Come quickly, David!' shouted his brother.
'Come to the feast!'

The boy was full of joy, for he longed to go with his brothers. He ran after him gladly, and came before Samuel, his cheeks red with running, his eyes bright.

'Now here is the boy whom God has chosen,' Samuel thought. So he went to David and blessed him. When he was old enough, David would be king over all the people.

Then the feast was held, and David joined in, happy but puzzled. He did not know why Samuel had asked for him to come, but he liked the old man.

After the feast Samuel went home, and David went back to his sheep. It was not time for him to be king. He was only a boy.

But he was a boy that everyone knew and loved. Sometimes he played to his sheep, leading them. from place to place, and they loved him and followed him.

David was a good shepherd. He guarded his flocks well. He had a sling and with it he could hurl a stone a long way and make it hit its mark.

When a lion and a bear came to kill his sheep, David sprang up and ran at them. He killed the lion, and then he killed the bear. He was the bravest of all the brothers, though he was the youngest.

Samuel often sent for David. He taught him the laws of God, and told him to obey them, for then he would be a wise and good ruler.

Then he would send David back to his sheep, and the boy would think of all he had learnt. He would make songs and sing them, while his sheep nibbled the grass and listened.

Saul was still the king of Israel. But he was an unhappy man; sometimes fits of madness came over him.

Then he would call for music to be played, for that was the only thing that brought him peace. His servants feared to see him so sad and gloomy.

One day one of them spoke to him: 'Won't you have someone to play upon the harp? I know a youth who would please you greatly. He is David, a son of Jesse the farmer.'

Then messengers were sent to Jesse. 'Our master, King Saul, commands you to send to him your son David,' they said.

So David got ready to go to the king. He took his harp with him. Soon he was standing before poor, unhappy Saul.

Saul liked David at once. 'You must stay with me and be my armour-bearer,' he said. 'You shall play and sing to me when I am troubled.'

So David stayed with Saul the King, and when he played upon his harp, the King forgot his sadness and was glad.

The Giant, Goliath

David stayed with Saul for a time and then went back to his father's sheep. One day his brothers told him that their old enemies, the Philistines, had come to fight against them once more.

'Three of us are going to fight them,' his brothers told him. 'If we want food, we will send word, and you must bring us bread and cheeses.'

David watched his brothers go. When the message came that they wanted food, he was glad. Now he would be able to see the enemy – and perhaps even watch a battle. He took food with him and went over the hills to find his brothers.

Now, as he talked with his brothers, David saw an amazing sight. In the Philistines' camp was a giant called Goliath. He was an enormous man, tall and broad and strong.

Every day he marched out of the camp, dressed in a coat of mail and a great helmet of brass. In front of him marched a man carrying his great shield, and in the giant's hand was a long spear.

The giant shouted at the top of his loud voice, 'Bring me a man to fight with! If he kills me, then the Philistines shall be your servants. If I kill him, you shall be ours and serve us. Where is the army of Israel? Can you not send one man to fight me?'

The Israelites were afraid of this giant. No one went to fight him. Some even ran away when he appeared. David was amazed to hear him, and to see the fear on his brothers' faces.

'Who will go to fight this giant?' asked David. But no man went.

'How dare he defy us!' cried David. 'I will go to fight him myself! '

King Saul heard his words and laughed. 'You are only a boy,' he said, 'and this man has been a soldier for years.'

'I have killed a lion and a bear,' said David. 'God will help me against this Philistine too.'

'Then go,' said Saul, and gave him armour. David put on a coat of mail and a heavy helmet, and strapped a great sword to his side.

'I cannot walk in these,' said David, and took them off. He picked up his stick and went down to the brook and chose five smooth stones. He put them into his shepherd's bag. Then he took his sling and went to meet the giant Goliath.

Down the opposite hillside came the giant. He saw that David carried a staff and he laughed.

'Am I a dog, to be beaten with a stick!' he roared.

Then David ran towards the giant, putting one of the smooth, round stones into his sling as he went. He flung the stone at the giant with all his might.

It hit Goliath in the middle of his forehead. The stone sank in and killed the giant. He fell down on his face, dead. David ran to him, took up his sword and cut off the giant's head. A cry of fear went up from the watching Philistines. They fled away in dismay, and Saul's men ran down the hillside to chase them.

It was a great victory for Israel. David was a hero; King Saul praised and rewarded him.

'Return no more to your sheep,' he said. 'Stay with me and I will make you a captain in my army.'

So David stayed with Saul. His great friend was Jonathan, the king's own son. The two were closer than brothers.

David soon became a great captain, leader of all Saul's men. Saul loved him and spoke well of him. But one day he turned against him.

There had been another victory, and the women went out to meet David, singing songs of praise. Saul heard the words and was angry.

'Saul has slain his thousands, and David his ten thousands!' sang the women.

These words made Saul jealous.

Then Saul lost all his love for David and made up his mind to kill him. At times David had to flee from Saul. Then Jonathan would miss David very much.

After a time Saul made his peace with David, and David came back to his palace. Jonathan wept with joy to see him again. David took his harp and often played to Saul when sadness came over him.

But one day, as David was sitting playing to him, Saul suddenly took up a spear and flung it at the young man. It did not hit him, but struck the wall. David ran from the room and would go to Saul no more.

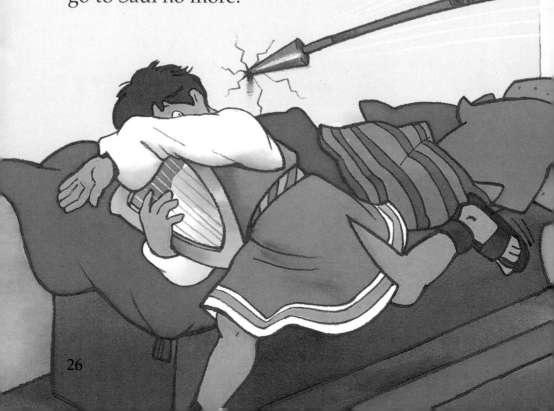

There came a great battle with the Philistines, in which Saul and his sons went to fight. Then sad news was brought to David.

'Saul the King is killed, and all his sons – Jonathan with them,' said the messenger. David wept for Jonathan his friend, whom he had loved so much.

'You shall be our king,' said the people of Israel to David. 'You shall rule over us and lead us in battle!'

And so David, who had been a shepherd-boy, became King of Israel, and ruled for many years.